STANLEY TIMBRE

How To Pray For Your Future Wife

A Daily Guide To Scripture Based Prayer

Contents

INTRODUCTION

Even if you haven't yet found your future bride, you can still pray for her protection and blessing before you even meet her. We have many attacks going on right now because we won't pray for the future. Before starting a marriage, it is a smart idea to pray to the Lord. If our world is to change, we need strong prayer warriors in the war room. A lack of prayer is the main cause of the issues the church is currently experiencing. Use this book to improve your prayer life. Maybe you've had several failed relationships because God didn't intend for you to be with these particular ladies. There is still hope for you because the future is full of rewards, but it is up to you to decide how your life will turn out.

You long for a God-fearing woman, not a destiny-destroyer. Jezebel served as an illustration of what a woman shouldn't be. Numerous powerful women are shown in the Bible, including Queen Esther, Jael, Zipporah, Rebecca, etc. Additionally, we can observe certain evil females, such as Athaliah, Herodias, Potiphar's wife, Delilah, etc. But Jezebel rises above these depraved women since she murdered numerous godly prophets, put Elijah the great prophet in danger, led a depraved life, tainted the country of Israel, and did many other evil deeds.

Jezebel encouraged King Ahab to turn away from Yahweh's

worship and promote that of the gods Baal and Asherah. Pray for the release of the future woman who is soon to enter your home. When she emulates God's generosity and freely contributes to others while keeping in mind that God will provide for her needs, she may experience financial breakthroughs.

Many women are severely constrained by stigma and harmful influences. If they are not set free before beginning a marital adventure, it will be harmful.

1

THANKSGIVING PRAYERS

You must give thanks to God for all that He has done and will do in your life as you prepare to pray for your future wife. God will do more for us in abundance if we give him thanks for what he has already done. Always pray the following prayers each day, and have faith that God will work wonders;

DAY 1 (THANKSGIVING)

Lord, I appreciate everything you've done for me. I give you all praise and gratitude for keeping me safe, Lord. (2 Samuel 22:3-4) My God, my rock, in whom I take refuge, my shield, and the horn of my salvation, my stronghold and my refuge, my savior; you save me from violence. I praise the Lord, who is worthy to be praised, and who saved me from my enemies.

Thank the All-Powerful for everything He has given you in life, including the food you consume, the people you greet, the love in your heart, and that great beginning. for his love. (Psalm 106:1) Praise the Lord. Give thanks to the Lord, for he is good; his love endures forever.

Thank you for your incredible influence on our lives and for the positive things you have done for us. (Psalm 9:1) Lord, I will praise you with all my heart and tell of all your wonderful works.

We are grateful that you can give us hope in the darkest of times and empower us to serve your purposes. My strength comes from the Sovereign Lord, who gives me deer-like feet and gives me the ability to walk on heights. (Habakkuk 3:19)

I appreciate all of your love and concern. I'm grateful for your grace and mercy. We are grateful for your constant presence and promise to never abandon us. We sincerely appreciate everything you gave up so that we could live in freedom. (Galatians 5:1) "It is for freedom that Christ has set us free. Stand firm, then, and do not let yourselves be burdened again by a yoke of slavery."

Please pardon us when we don't express our gratitude to you enough for who you are, what you do, and what you've given. (Psalm 86:5) "You, Lord, are forgiving and good, abounding in love to all who call to you." Help us to set our eyes and our hearts on you afresh.

Renew our spirits, fill us with your peace and joy. We love you and we need you, this day and every day. We give you praise and thanks, for You alone are worthy! In Jesus' Name, Amen."

2

PRAYERS FOR FUTURE WIFE'S SAFETY

There is much good and evil in the world today, and the Devil has stolen many noble souls. The Lord is our refuge. You must formally request God's protection over the woman he is about to introduce to you. The following prayer points will help you as you fervently and seriously pray;

Day 2 (PRAYERS FOR FUTURE WIFE'S SAFETY)

All who pray to You are protected, O God of Heaven's Armies. I beg You to keep the woman I hope to marry safe. (Psalms 5:11) But let all who take refuge in you be glad; let them ever sing for joy. Spread your protection over them, that those who love your name may rejoice in you. Father, Wherever my future wife is now, may she be safe. Keep her from danger.

I pray for protection from actual dangers to her health, including the prevention of accidents, natural disasters, and those who would harm her. (Psalms 46:1) God is our refuge and strength, an ever-present help in trouble. Heavenly Father, Keep her in Your mighty hand. I ask these things in Jesus' mighty name. Amen.

Lord, please keep her mind safe. Father, the mentality of the flesh is one of death, but the mentality of the Spirit is one of life and peace. (Romans 8:6) O God, set our mind on You. Let us not be conformed to this world, but be transformed by the renewing of our minds that we may prove what Your will is, that which is good and acceptable and perfect.

By the power of Your Spirit, help her to focus on what is true, what is honorable, what is right, what is beautiful, what is reputable, and what is pure (Romans 12:2)

God, strengthen her with the might of Your power. Dress her in Your armor so that she can withstand the devil's ploys. (Ephesians 6:10-12)

Day 3 (PRAYERS FOR FUTURE WIFE'S SAFETY)

Lord, you are our guardian; you are the shadow on our right hand. Keep our souls safe and shield us from all harm. Observe both our entrance and exit. From now on and always. Amen, in the name of Jesus.

Lord, send your angels to watch over her as she sleeps so that

HOW TO PRAY FOR YOUR FUTURE WIFE

no harm will come to her.

I implore the holy spirit to direct her choices in life. Amen. She won't make bad decisions. (Deuteronomy 31 vs 6) Be strong and courageous. Do not be afraid or terrified because of them, for the LORD your God goes with you; he will never leave you nor forsake you."

Lord, Amen. Protect her from wolves in sheep's clothing, evil advice, and bad friends who thwart her destiny. 1 Corinthians 5:11-12, Proverbs 1:10-13

Day 4 (PRAYERS FOR FUTURE WIFE'S SAFETY)

Oh God, protect her from all territorial demons that could hinder her progress. Ephessians 6:10-20, Rom 13:11-14 and Dear Lord, Guide her from every territorial demon monitoring her success

Protect her heart from any suicidal thoughts brought on by anxiety and depression. 2 Timothy 1 vs 7, Isaiah 37 vs 4

Oh my God! You assured us—your children—that we would live long enough to carry out your wishes. (1 Corinthians 15:55; Psalm 68:20) Father, She won't ever meet an untimely demise because you'll keep her safe for your work. Amen

Day 5 (PRAYERS FOR FUTURE WIFE'S SAFETY)

Father, wherever they may be, guard her family against all the ills of the day and whatever difficulties they may encounter. John 16:33 and Psalm 34:19

Father, In the name of Jesus, save her from falling into the hands of evil. Job 9 vs 22-24

Father, In the name of Jesus, protect her from spirits that steal her joy. (2 Thessalonians 3 vs 3) But the Lord is faithful. He will establish you and guard you against the evil one.

In Jesus' name, I pray that every hand that reaches out to touch her future withers. No weapon formed against you will be successful, and you will refute every tongue raised in judgment against you. (Isaiah 54 vs 17) No weapon that is fashioned against you shall succeed, and you shall confute every tongue that rises against you in judgment. This is the heritage of the servants of the Lord and their vindication from me, declares the Lord."

Dear God, in the name of Jesus, Amen, cast out every spirit that tries to oppress her. Psalm 23 vs 1 - 6.

In the name of Jesus, the Almighty Lord grants her complete deliverance wherever she may be. Call on me in times of difficulty. Psalms 50:15 - And call upon me in the day of trouble: I will deliver thee, and thou shalt glorify me.

7

3

PRAYERS FOR FUTURE WIFE'S GOOD ATTITUDE

Marrying a negative lady is a risky proposition. A negative mindset destroys a home while a positive attitude strengthens it. You are to pray for her in this chapter so that the Lord may grant her a godly character. The following prayer points will help you as you fervently and seriously pray;

Day 6 (PRAYERS FOR FUTURE WIFE'S GOOD ATTITUDE)

Good and true Savior, You gaze in the heart rather than at the outside aspect. I hope that words like kind, faithful, dependable, and honest will be used to describe my future wife as I wonder about her. Galatians 5:22–23

People will praise her for being a Godly person when talking about her. Lord, make her heart's integrity shine like a priceless ruby.

She will be developed as a result of her training and life experiences. Use it all to help her develop into a Godly woman in the name of Jesus.

I pray to you for a wife, not a blade. I, therefore, disapprove of every sexist and haughty woman in my vicinity. (Proverbs 14:) "A wise woman builds her home, but a foolish woman tears it down with her own hands."

Everlasting Father, I ask for a respectful wife who will uphold the dignity of my home. (Ephesians 5:22–24) In Jesus' name, I cast out of her every demon of arrogance.

In Jesus' name, I beg you, Father, to keep her from being possessed by the spirit of Jezebel, which could be trying to wreck my life and the lives of other divinely gifted men.

Day 7 (PRAYERS FOR FUTURE WIFE'S GOOD ATTITUDE)

In the name of Jesus, Father, make her a good wife who will give my parents peace of mind. Whoever finds a wife finds a good thing and wins the Lord's favor, according to Proverbs 18:22 (KJV).

Make her a wonderful mother and wife who will look after my

mother and any future children.

Father, in the name of Jesus, make her a woman of virtue Psalm 31:27–28 She pays attention to how her family behaves and avoids eating idleness for breakfast. Her husband also praises her, and her children stand up to bless her.

Father in heaven, In Jesus' name, make her a woman of moral character who will have a positive influence on my future children.

Please, God, make her heart tender. In the name of Jesus, keep her from becoming a narcissist or a manipulator. Don't give me a woman who will make me feel anxious. Amen. Leviticus 25:17 Do not take advantage of each other, but fear your God.

In Jesus' name, Father, make her a role model for other women in the community as a wife.

Day 8 (PRAYERS FOR FUTURE WIFE'S GOOD ATTITUDE)

Father, make her a woman who will bring my family together and bring harmony (Genesis 3:15, Ruth 4:11, Luke 1:38, I Timothy 2:15)

Father lord, Help her not to be nonchalant to everything that concerns me and my family in Jesus Name. 1 Corinthians 7

Make her an angel, a woman of miracles who will bless me and my future offspring, O Lord.

Father, I need a woman in my life who will act like a wife, mother, and sister. Amen. Proverbs 18:22 (KJV) "Whoso findeth a wife findeth a good thing, and obtaineth favour of the Lord."

4

PRAYERS FOR FUTURE WIFE'S BOND WITH GOD

It's important to realize that the woman you want in your home needs to have a solid relationship with God. In the marriage equation, we are powerless to override God. Because neither the wife nor the husband has a God-fearing mindset, many marriages fail. Please pay close attention when you pray the following requests for her in-depth relationship with God:

Day 9 (PRAYERS FOR FUTURE WIFE'S BOND WITH GOD)

Lord, provide me a woman who fears You and is Loving, Caring, Understanding, and Reliable. KJV PROVERBS 31:11-12 KJV
   "The heart of her husband doth safely trust in her, so that he shall have no need of spoil. She will do him good and not evil all the days of her life."

In the name of Jesus, Father, utilize her mighty in your vineyard.

In the name of Jesus, Father, keep her soul under your care daily and keep her from harboring sinful thoughts.Galatians 5:19–21, James 1:14–15

In the name of Jesus, Father, grant her the ability to live according to your will and refrain from pursuing worldly goals. Colossians 3:2–4

In the name of Jesus, Father, make her your friend so she can follow you. (Revelation 3:20, ESV) Behold, I stand at the door and knock. If anyone hears my voice and opens the door, I will come in to him and eat with him, and he with me. What a friend we have in Jesus, All our sins and griefs to bear!

Father, may the sacrifice made by your son Jesus Christ on the cross at Calvary not be in vain for her. Amen.

Day 10 (PRAYERS FOR FUTURE WIFE'S BOND WITH GOD)

In the name of Jesus, Father, deliver her from the advice of the wicked. Psalm 1 vs 1 & 2

Father, do not let her go astray and fall by the wayside. "My people have become lost sheep; Their shepherds have led them astray. ... And have forgotten their resting place. Jeremiah 50:5

In the name of Jesus, Father, establish your word into her heart.

Colossians 2:6–7 (NIV).

In the name of Jesus, fortify her heart, soul, and body for your works. Psalm 46:1–3, Psalm 119:28, and Isaiah 40:29–31

In the name of Jesus, Father, make her a lady of faith when difficulties arise. Job 13:15; Matthew 15:28;

Dear God, I recognize that many women worry about the future. Please give her the courage to speak positively about it rather than negatively, as Proverbs 18:21 states, "Death and life are in the power of the tongue."

Day 11 (PRAYERS FOR FUTURE WIFE'S BOND WITH GOD)

In the name of Jesus, ask God to deliver her from any concern or pessimism. You have not succumbed to any temptation that is not common to man.

In the name of Jesus, Father, save her from temptations that might occur during difficult times. (1 Corinthians 10:13). God is faithful, and he will not let you be tempted beyond your ability, but with the temptation, he will also provide the way of escape, that you may be able to endure it"

Father ,I ask for a close fellowship with my future wife. Do not forsake her in all her endeavors Isaiah 43:25-26, Leviticus 26:11 Moreover, I will make My dwelling among you, and My soul will not reject you.

Father, may she always be a burning example of your good works (1 Peter 1:22-23). (Isa 55:10–11)

5

PRAYERS FOR FUTURE WIFE'S STUDIES

I assure you that you will require an intellectual woman with a strong academic background to raise your children. If things go wrong, academics can be tough and frustrating. You'll need to ask the Lord for an excellent spirit for her. These prayers will guide you in the correct direction;

Day 12 (PRAYERS FOR FUTURE WIFE'S STUDIES)

Father in heaven, I give You thanks for my education and the courses I have taken. I ask that You give my future wife the inspiration and motivation she needs to pursue her studies with clarity.

Please direct her to the appropriate training, and may she enjoy her academic endeavors. Assist her in studying morally with the knowledge that all she does is for Your honor. Proverbs 16:3; Daniel 6:3

Dear Everlasting Father, Make sure she has a retentive memory so she can learn and remember what she learns. I am aware that you never leave her side. Amen. Isaiah 11:2

Father, in the name of Jesus, give her the wisdom she needs to apply it to all of her academic challenges.

Lord, fill her with the spirit of excellence so that she can surpass her colleagues in the name of Jesus. Proverbs 22:29, Daniel 6:3,

Father, favor her among her colleagues when she least expects your divine touch, in the name of Jesus.

Day 13 (PRAYERS FOR FUTURE WIFE'S STUDIES)

In the name of Jesus, I bind every spirit of forgetfulness and indolence in her academics, dear God.

In the name of Jesus, Father, nothing will prevent her from pursuing her academic goals.

Dear God, I ask that you guide her toward academic excellence and open her eyes to the plans you have for her. Psalm 119 vs 105

Lord Jesus, give her the courage to pursue her dreams and to advance in her studies (Isaiah 40:31)

Father, I ask you to give her a positive attitude in her academics today. She must approach everything she does with optimism. Amen

To ensure that she stays on track academically, Father channeled her mind to always act appropriately at the appropriate time. John 7 vs 1–13

Day 14 (PRAYERS FOR FUTURE WIFE'S STUDIES)

Father, Free her mind of any emotional stress that might interfere with her studies and prevent her from performing to the best of her ability. Psalm 28 vs 7 "The LORD is my strength and my shield; in him my heart trusts, and I am helped; my heart exults, and with my song I give thanks to him."

Dear God, protect her from the enemy's vices that could attempt to steal her outstanding spirit. Psalm 21 vs 11, Psalm 37:7 Rest in the Lord and wait patiently for Him; Do not fret because of him who prospers in his way, Because of the man who carries out wicked schemes.

Father, support her in developing her sense of worth so she can feel confident and valued in her academics. 2 Timothy 1:7, "For God gave us a spirit not of fear but of power and love and self-control.

Please, in the name of Jesus, grant her divine inspiration so that she can excel in all that she does academically.

6

PRAYERS FOR FUTURE WIFE'S LOVE FOR OTHERS

You require a woman who is compassionate toward others. a woman who is loving, caring, and inspires others in her society. Most people respect and honor such women. If your wife is unkind to others, it could have an impact on you because you might come under suspicion. May you not be held accountable for your spouse's errors. Amen. Your future will be secured if you offer the following prayers;

Day 15 (PRAYERS FOR HER LOVE FOR OTHERS)

My Savior, Jesus According to Your Word. A person who is born of God and loves other people. I hope my future wife will share this trait of loving those around her. Deuteronomy 15:7-8 "If anyone is poor among your fellow Israelites in any of the towns of the land the Lord your God is giving you, do not be hardhearted or tightfisted toward them. Rather, be openhanded and freely lend them whatever they need."

Oh my God! Give her a compassionate heart that is moved by the plight of others. May she always be a woman who inspires me to show compassion to others as well. Make her a shining example of how to follow the command to love your neighbor as yourself. Amen. Matthew 5:16 "In the same way, let your light shine before others, that they may see your good deeds and glorify your Father in heaven."

Father, please provide her with the necessary social skills to engage with good people.

Father in heaven, grant her a spirit of moderation that will enable her to handle social situations. Galatians 5.22 ESV And beside this, giving all diligence, add to your faith virtue; and to virtue knowledge; And to knowledge temperance; and to temperance patience; and to patience godliness; And to godliness brotherly kindness; and to brotherly kindness charity.

God, please assist her to gain the knowledge, wisdom, and insight she needs to handle any challenging problems that may emerge in her community. For the Lord gives wisdom; from his mouth come knowledge and understanding. (Proverbs 2:6).

Day 16 (PRAYERS FOR HER LOVE FOR OTHERS)

Assist her in inspiring and motivating others to advance in all facets of life.

Lord, may you grant her a forgiving spirit so that she can forget those who have wronged her. Ephesians 4:31, Ephesians 4:26-27, Colossians 3:13.

Oh my God! Give her the discernment to choose her friends wisely and to act in your favor. Jeremiah 23:16-22, Acts 5:3, Matthew 16:17

Father, protect her from demoralizing individuals and those who would tempt her to hell. Philippians 4:6-7, Psalm 1 vs 1.

Father God, lead her closer to the person who will support her in achieving greatness in life and serve as her destined aid. (Proverbs 17:17) A friend loves at all times, and a brother is born for a time of adversity.

Please, God, make her receptive to wise counsel from her loved ones.

Day 17 (PRAYERS FOR HER LOVE FOR OTHERS)

Father, may you provide her the grace to absorb all the wonderful moral teachings that her loved ones and parents have imparted to her.

In the name of Jesus, Father God, protect her heart from any aggressive spirits so that she won't cause trouble for the community. Proverbs 28:17 A man that doeth violence to the blood of [any] person shall flee to the pit; let no man stay him.

Father, protect her from harlots and narrow-minded friends, as well as from those who would destroy her spiritual life.

Father, save her from pals who are scheming to do her harm while she assists others from all over the world. Proverbs 16 vs 27-29

Heavenly Father, please grant my future bride the role of sister, mother, and greatest friend in my life. Make her a woman who will develop a love for my family and me.

Dear God, protect her from falling in love with the things of this world and abandoning your kingdom.

Make her a preacher and a doer in your world, Father. She needs the wisdom to populate your kingdom, so grant it to her. Amen. James 1 vs 22 NLV "But don't just listen to God's word. You must do what it says. Otherwise, you are only fooling yourselves."

7

PRAYERS FOR MY FUTURE WIFE'S FAMILY

When you are married, you essentially get married to everyone and everything in that person's life. That is one unknown fact about young adults that many still don't know. You might be impacted in some manner if something bad happens to her family. God will grant your requests if you fervently pray the following prayers;

Day 18 (PRAYERS FOR MY FUTURE WIFE'S FAMILY)

I make a prayer to Jehovah, my God, for my future wife's family. I pray for every relationship she has, Lord, even though I do not yet know who they are. O God, keep them secure in your care.

Father in heaven, I ask that they be united in the unity that your love creates today. Ephesians 4:13

Lord, may her parents set a good example for the kind of relationship I desire to have with her. "Love the Lord your God with all your heart and with all your soul and with all your strength and with all your mind; and, love your neighbor as yourself" (Luke 10:27).

Please help her to love her family with wisdom. The name of Jesus. Amen.

In the magnificent name of Jesus, Father, make them your special people (Deuteronomy 14:2, 1 Peter 2:9).

Father, keep them free from ailments and diseases so they can live out the remainder of their days in perfect peace.

Lord, you are the prince of peace; in the name of Jesus, stop every raging storm in her household. Rom. 6:23.

Day 19 (PRAYERS FOR MY FUTURE WIFE'S FAMILY)

Heavenly Father, Help them to develop a more profound love for you, Father, so they can continue to love you for all of eternity.

Father, I cover them all in the priceless blood of your Son, Jesus, who will protect them from any danger.

If there are any narcissists among them, you are the Lord who has the power to move monarchs. Lord, please change a narcissist's heart and make them as kind as doves. Amen

Father, in the name of Jesus, extend their coast in all aspects of life.

Oh my God! In the name of Jesus, deliver them from the wolves that are hiding as sheeps.

Day 20 (PRAYERS FOR MY FUTURE WIFE'S FAMILY)

In the name of Jesus, Father, I pray that they will not abandon you and your works.

Father, please help them to always focus on you, the source and summit of our faith. Amen

O Lord, grant them in her family everlasting joy. Amen

Please, God, make it possible for them to benefit from Quick Solution in all aspects of their lives. Amen

8

PRAYERS FOR MY FUTURE WIFE'S HEALTH

The fact that people pass away every day from one disease or another is not news. Even though you should love your husband in sickness and in health, if the devil gives your spouse a serious disease, there will be no way for you to enjoy your marriage. Offer these prayers for your future wife's health;

Day 21 (PRAYERS FOR MY FUTURE WIFE'S HEALTH)

Jesus, the Great Physician, You are our supporter and provide us with life through Your Spirit. Keep my future wife healthy under Your caring touch. Keep her healthy and away from any diseases and problems.

I ask that You speedily heal her even if she gets sick.

I also pray that her living circumstances will support her health.

Lord, spare her the burden of sickness. I appreciate that You have the authority to do so. You are our physician. Amen.

Dear God, I forbid any hypertensive news; in the name of Jesus, her ears shall not be exposed to harmful announcements.

Day 22 (PRAYERS FOR MY FUTURE WIFE'S HEALTH)

In the name of Jesus, the incurable illness won't strike her. Amen.

The mighty hand of the Holy Spirit, flush out every secret disease in her body, Amen.

In the name of Jesus, I also free her from all generational diseases and curses. Galatians 3:13 ESV Christ redeemed us from the curse of the law by becoming a curse for us—for it is written, "Cursed is everyone who is hanged on a tree"

By the power of the Holy Ghost, I eliminate every illness that the Devil had prepared for her on the day of her joy. Amen

Dear Father, every sickness she brought on herself. In the name of Jesus, Father, have mercy on her and free her. Amen. 3 John 1:2
"Beloved, I wish above all things that thou mayest prosper

and be in health, even as thy soul prospereth."

You created us in your likeness, God. Father, everything she possesses that desires to thwart her destiny you did not create. In the name of Jesus, I ask that your strong hands cast them out. Amen.

9

PRAYERS FOR FUTURE WIFE'S CAREER

I t is crucial to pray for your prospective wife's professional success. It's advantageous for a couple to have stable careers that provide for the family's needs. You don't want to risk your marriage to poverty. Pray the following for her job with all of your strength;

Day 23 (PRAYERS FOR FUTURE WIFE'S CAREER)

You direct our actions in everything, Name above all Names. May You direct the path taken by the woman You have ordered me to marry, leading her into the correct line of work. Isaiah 30:21

21 Whether you turn to the right or to the left, your ears will hear a voice behind you, saying, "This is the way; walk in it. Psalms 84:11 For the LORD God is a sun and shield; the LORD

bestows favor and honor; no good thing does he withhold from those whose walk is blameless.

I beg that it be a happy and fulfilling one for her as well as one that provides for her.

Prepare her actions to win the favor of her co-workers and the respect of the people she works with.

Help her use her employment as a tool to serve the kingdom while preventing her from idolizing her profession. Amen. 1 Corinthians 10:7 Do not be idolaters, as some of them were; as it is written: "The people sat down to eat and drink and got up to indulge in revelry."

In the great name of Jesus, Father, grant her the ability to reap the rewards of her labor. You will eat the fruit of your labor; blessings and prosperity will be yours." (Psalm 123:2 NIV)

Give her the courage, O Lord, to proclaim your kingdom to her superiors in the name of Jesus.

Day 24 (PRAYERS FOR FUTURE WIFE'S CAREER)

In the name of Jesus, Lord Jesus, the Devil will not steal her benefits. Amen. Philippians 4:19, Numbers 6:24–26

Almighty God, In Jesus' name, make her an example of a virtue-filled woman at work. Proverbs 21:9, Proverbs 31:26 She opens her mouth with wisdom, and the teaching of kindness is on her tongue.

Make her a confident lady who speaks well about her career because, as we all know, words have power. Save her from her fears. Amen

In the powerful name of Jesus, Father, I pray that she will not be the cause of her Job's abrupt termination. In Jesus' name, she won't be implicated at work.

Dear God, may Her Job and the blessings you give her not distract her from serving your kingdom in the name of Jesus. Colossians 4:2, John 15:5–6

Day 25 (PRAYERS FOR FUTURE WIFE'S CAREER)

According to your message, it will be difficult for the wealthy to enter God's kingdom. In the name of Jesus, Heavenly Father, I ask that you grant her benefits that will save her from going down the road to damnation.

In Jesus' name, Father, grant her complete career peace. Isaiah 26:3 "You will keep in perfect peace those whose minds are steadfast, because they trust in you."

In Jesus' name, she would reach out to potential narcissistic bosses nearby to win their hearts so as to make her job easier for her.

In the name of Jesus, Father God, I pray that she won't make any costly errors in her career. Amen. John 8:32 "And ye shall know the truth, and the truth shall make you free." It is the spirit of error that will make a Christian indulge in fornication or adultery continuously and still believe he or she is on the right path to heaven.

10

A PRAYER FOR THE FRIENDS OF
MY FUTURE WIFE

A person just needs one good buddy to make their life successful, just as they only need one bad corporation to ruin their lives. The appropriate company will make your future wife's life delightful. God will send her good friends if you pray with the following requests:

Day 26 (PRAYERS FOR FUTURE WIFE'S FRIENDS)

God of mercy, thank you for creating us to live in society. I desire for my future wife to have a strong social network. The Godly should carefully select their friends, according to Proverbs.

May she be loved and cared for by her friends during the highs and lows of life. I hope they are a source of knowledge and provide her with a sense of humor as she remains in their company. I request wise advice from them. I appreciate the gift of your friendship. Amen

Lord, protect her from wolves that are posing as sheep. Amen

Save her from friends who will tempt her to follow the path of destruction.

Father, protect her from friends who will rob her of her joy. Amen

Day 27 (PRAYERS FOR FUTURE WIFE'S FRIENDS)

Heavenly Father, Give her a buddy who will help her reach the heights of brilliance. Amen

Father in heaven, please provide her with a buddy who will help her grow spiritually and lift her. Amen

Father, please give her the divine understanding to cooperate even with the appropriate friends. AMEN

Day 28 (PRAYERS FOR FUTURE WIFE'S FRIENDS)

In the name of Jesus, direct her to the appropriate church that will impart your unadulterated teachings and that which will help her develop a strong spiritual life.

In the name of Jesus, Father, please help her to care for her pastors in your vineyards.

Lord Almighty, make use of her powerfully in your vineyard so that she can spread righteousness in God's church.

I hope that when Your Word is preached week by week, she will learn more about You. I want her to be encouraged to love and do good things, and I want her to encourage people in return.

May her church be a place where she can find stability and strength during difficult times, as well as a place to rejoice during prosperous ones. Father God, thank You. Amen.

11

PRAYERS FOR FUTURE WIFE'S FINANCE

J ust as you have prayed for her job, so you don't want to risk letting poverty enter your life. I hope that you are encouraged to cling to the potent truths in these Scriptures as you continue to pray for a breakthrough in your future wife's financial situation. What a blessing it is to understand that God is the true owner of everything and that he has graciously entrusted the care of the earth to us. May she give generously with a heart of thanksgiving for his goodness as you pray for her financial well-being. Ask the Lord to grant her continued blessings through these prayer points;

Day 29 (PRAYERS FOR FUTURE WIFE'S FINANCE)

Thank you, Lord, for creating the earth, the heavens, and everything that resides in them. You have everything, both wealth and honor are yours! Please help her to understand that everything she needs comes from you as I pray for financial success in her life. Being a gracious God, you freely give and provide for all of her needs. Amen.

Thank you, Lord, for generously meeting all of her needs following your riches in glory (Philippians 4:19).

Help her to believe that you will provide for her and my family and meet their wants because you are the God who provides for the birds of the sky.

As I bring my request for her financial breakthrough before your seat of grace, I thank you, Lord, that she may rely on you to provide for her. Amen.

Lord, help her to freely give to you and to those around her in return for all that you have freely given to her.

Help her to give wisely and generously to those in need even amid financial hardship. According to Your Word, those who are generous will prosper, and those who refresh others will also be refreshed (Proverbs 11:25). Thank you for allowing her to share from the plenty and fullness you have provided for her. Amen.

Lord, thank you for setting aside a place in glory for her! Encourage her to keep in mind that there is more to life than just the tangible objects of this world. She will inherit all the eternal blessings from your Word when she sees you face to face. That will be such a beautiful day!

Help her to faithfully serve you on this planet in the knowledge that she will receive rewards in heaven that are unimaginable to her. I hope she hears you say, "Well done, good and faithful servant," someday. Amen. Matthew 25:23 "His master replied, 'Well done, good and faithful servant! You have been faithful with a few things; I will put you in charge of many things. Come and share your master's happiness! '

12

PRAYERS FOR MYSELF

Yes, you must pray for yourself for your future wife to find you in good shape. Prayer removes restrictions and yokes. You will require the Lord's complete deliverance. Say these prayers, and everything will be okay for you;

Day 30 (PRAYERS FOR MYSELF)

Lord, give me the stamina to hold fast to your word until she gets here. I ask for the ability to avoid sexual longing.

Sacred Father, To wait for the woman of my dreams, I beg for patience.

Lord, guide my steps so I can find my love.

Please give me the courage to approach her when I see her.

Amen.

In the name of Jesus, enrich my bank account so I can support my future bride. Amen

I come before your throne, Father, with a heavy heart and a worried mind. Your Holy Presence, fill me. Allow me to relax and enjoy the serenity. Permit me to sense your defense. Allow me to experience being protected by your wings. In you, I'm hidden, safe, and secure. Only you can offer and receive everything.

Father, I ask that you please remove my fear and grant me your indescribable serenity. My life is in your hands, as you are aware. Father, you alone are the source of my hope and trust.

PRAYERS FOR FUTURE MARRIAGE

You have prayed for both yourself and your future wife. Now is the moment to pray for your upcoming union so that the Lord will enter that household first. Here are some things to pray for:

Day 31 (PRAYERS FOR FUTURE MARRIAGE)

Father in heaven, The unforeseen threats to both my marriage and the marriages of other people weigh heavily on my heart.

41

There are so many things in this world that have the potential to devastate, harm, or rob us of our joy. I ask for protection for each of us so that no matter what happens, we will remain steadfast in our belief in Your plan for our lives.

In the name of Jesus, Amen, I also pray that our marriages will be more resilient than ever and able to withstand any threat.

Lord, I ask for Your protection of my future children on an emotional, physical, and spiritual level. Help them to trust You as their strength and refuge by keeping evil away from them. I ask that You protect their brains from false teaching and give them the wisdom to know the truth.

I pray that You will give my future children the fortitude and bravery to face danger knowing that You have triumphed and will one day right all injustice and wrong.

As they reside in the spiritual home You have provided for them, please help my future children to find comfort in Your shadow. Amen. Let them know that their residence on earth is only temporary and that the only place they can find safety is in Jesus.

Jesus, You are our stronghold, and this house is enclosed by walls of love. Our family finds refuge in the grace outlined in your words of truth because you are our sanctuary. We hold one another in the faith, hope, and joy you sent because you are our treasure. We bow down to you as our leader and find safety, goodness, and rest there. Lord, I thank you.

13

Other Books By The Author
(STANLEY TIMBRE)

H OW TO TREAT A WOMAN BETTER

HOW TO HEAL FROM EMOTIONAL ABUSE

Made in the USA
Las Vegas, NV
06 December 2023

82209064R00031